The Dad Appreciation Book:
A Creative Fill-In-The-Blank Venture

The Perfect Gift for Dad

Dad, My top 3 reasons
you are the best Dad ever:

1. _____

2. _____

3. _____

A father is a man who expects his son
to be as good a man as he is meant to be.

-Frank A. Clark

Dad,
You are my

_____

My father was my teacher. But most importantly he was a great dad.

-Beau Bridges

Dad,
I love how you

....

....

You need a strong family because
at the end, they will love you and support
you unconditionally. Luckily,
I have my dad, mom and sister.

-Esha Gupta

Dad,
I really love it when

_____

_____

Becoming a dad means you have to be a role model for your son and be someone he can look up to.

-Wayne Rooney

Dad,
My favorite memory of us
from the past year was when we

_____

_____

_____

The most important thing in the world is family and love.

-John Wooden

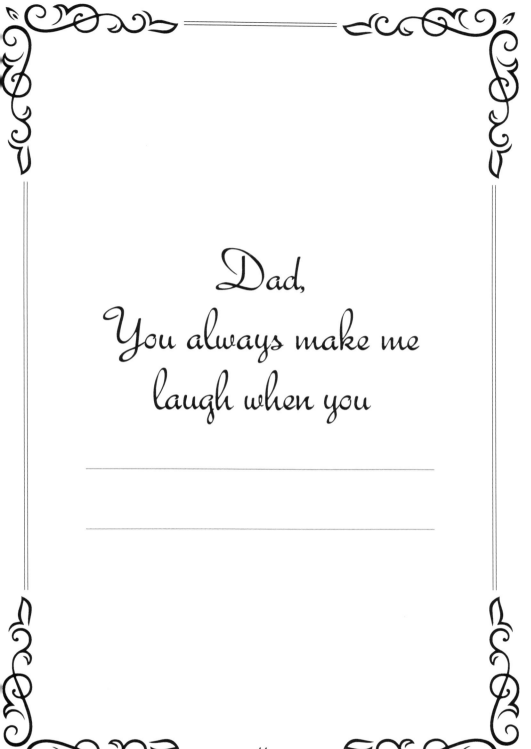

Dad,
You always make me
laugh when you

_____

_____

One of the greatest titles in the world is parent, and one of the biggest blessings in the world is to have parents to call mom and dad.

-Jim DeMint

Dad,
You always

_____

_____

_____

Anyone can be a father, but it takes someone special to be a dad, and that's why I call you dad, because you are so special to me. You taught me the game and you taught me how to play it right.

-Wade Boggs

Dad,
Thank you for

When a father gives to his son,
both laugh; when a son gives
to his father, both cry.

-Shakespeare

Dad,
You make me

_____

_____

_____

A real man loves his wife, and places his family as the most important thing in life. Nothing has brought me more peace and content in life than simply being a good husband and father.

-Frank Abagnale

I am so _____

to be able to call you

my Dad

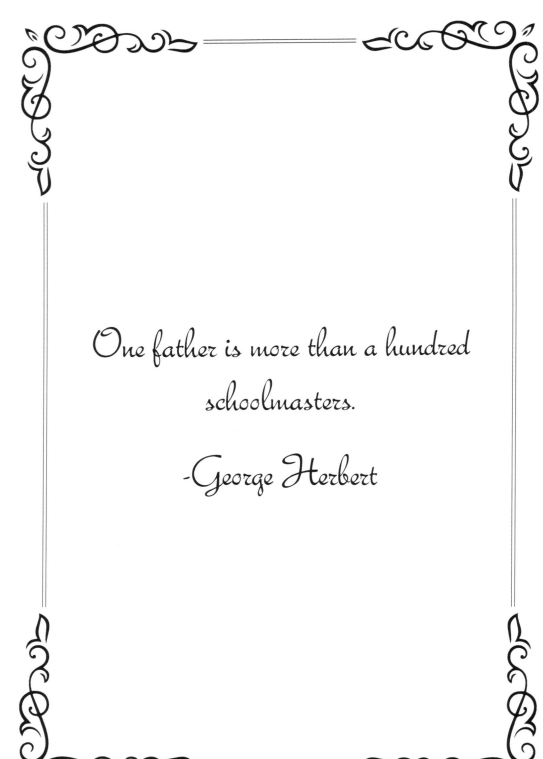

One father is more than a hundred
schoolmasters.

-George Herbert

Dad,
I'll never forget when

_____

_____

_____

_____

My father used to say that it's never too late to do anything you wanted to do. And he said, 'You never know what you can accomplish until you try.'

-Michael Jordan

Dad,
Thank you for instilling

_____

_____ in me.

It is a wise father that knows
his own child.

-Shakespeare

Dad,
Thanks for all the

_____

_____

_____

I'm so proud of you that it makes me proud of me. I hope you know that.

-John Green

Dad,
I will always love you
despite the fact you

_____

_____

As the Father has loved me,
so have I loved you.

-Jesus

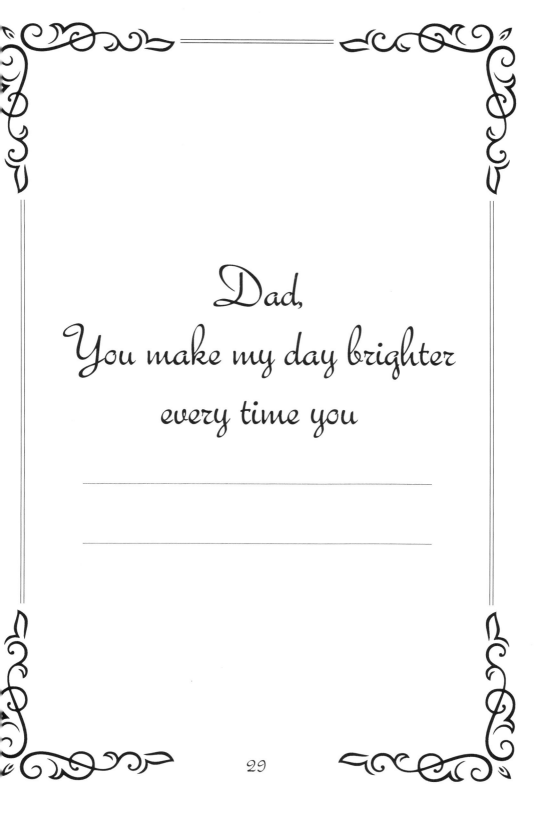

Dad,
You make my day brighter
every time you

_____

_____

There is no remedy for love
but to love more.

-Henry David Thoreau

Dad,
Without you I would

_____

_____

To her, the name of father
was another name for love.

-Fanny Fern

Dad,
Nobody can

---

quite like you

*My father didn't tell me how to live.
He lived and let me watch him do it.*

-Clarence Budington Kelland

Dad,
I admire your

_____

_____

Dads are most ordinary men turned
by love into heroes, adventurers,
story-tellers, and singers of song.

-Pam Brown

Dad,
Some people think you are
weird when you

_____, but I

know _____

A father is someone you look up to no matter how tall you have grown.

-Unknown

Dad,
I look forward to

_____

_____

I cannot think of any need
in childhood as strong as the need
for a father's protection.

-Sigmund Freud

Dad,
I love watching

_____

_____ with you

Any man can be a father, but it takes someone special to be a dad.

-Anne Geddes

Dad,
I love it when we talk about

_____

_____

It is not flesh and blood, but the heart which makes us fathers and sons.

-Johann Friedrich von Schiller

Dad,
I love that you always
_____ when
I'm having a bad day

45

It's only when you grow up and step back from him - or leave hi for your own home - it's only then that you can measure his greatness and fully appreciate it.

-Margaret Truman

Dad,

You inspire me to be
a better person because

_____

_____

The quality of a father can be seen in the goals, dreams, and aspirations he sets not only for himself but for his family.

-Reed Markham

Dad,
You are not only my

_____ , but also

my _____

He adopted a role called Being
a Father so that his child would
have something mythical and infinitely
important: a Protector.

-Tom Wolfe

Dad,
Mom sometimes says that
you _____, but I

_____

As the father of the President,
he could provide something different: the
love and support I needed to handle
the pressure of the job.

-George W. Bush

Dad,
You always make me
laugh when you

I pronounce it as certain that there was never yet a truly great man that was not at the same time truly virtuous.

-Benjamin Franklin

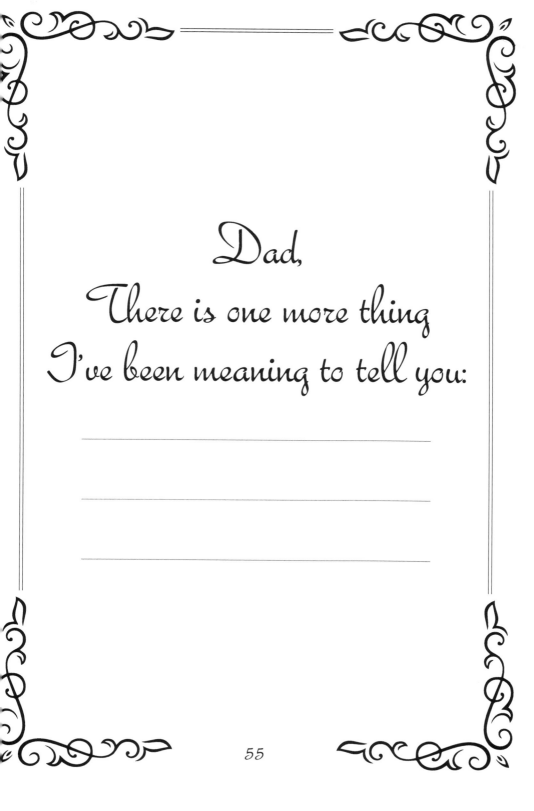

Dad,
There is one more thing
I've been meaning to tell you:

_____

_____

_____

What was silent in the father speaks in the son, and often I found in the son the unveiled secret of the father.

-Friedrich Nietzsche

Made in the USA
Lexington, KY
15 November 2017